THIS HOLIDAY JOURNAL BELONGS TO

A GIFT FROM

My Christmas Diary

A JOURNAL FOR THE
HOLIDAY SEASON
THROUGH THE YEARS

MARJORIE MERENA

AVON BOOKS · NEW YORK

AVON BOOKS, INC.
1350 Avenue of the Americas
New York, New York 10019

HOW TO USE
YOUR CHRISTMAS DIARY

This journal is for you to document and keep track of needs and events through the holiday season. It is divided into ten separate, yearly sections, plus a section in the back for Special Celebrations, such as a FIRST CHRISTMAS BIRTHDAY CELEBRATION. As you fill your journal, you may refer to previous Christmas entries at a glance, as well as note things to remember for future holiday seasons. Consult your Christmas diary when shopping, making plans, sending cards, entertaining; write down favorite crafts, recipes, and memories. The calendar included for each season begins with the earliest day Thanksgiving will fall on and continues through Twelfth Night. Schedule shopping trips as well as noting invitations or a holiday season birthday that could easily be forgotten. Each section offers ample space to keep lists, events, ideas, and comments that will be useful in the following years, as well as for the pasting in of photographs. Your Christmas diary not only guides you through each holiday season but is a treasured book of memories.

My great-aunts and great-uncles arrive first, Dora and George. Perfume and cold air fill the entryway. Then Pauline and Andrew with ever-present cigar. Grandma is busy in the kitchen. Daddy takes coats, and Mom couriers sacks and covered dishes to the kitchen. We are anxious to see our cousins from the suburbs.

My most treasured memories are the scents, sounds, and sensations that come to mind when I think of childhood celebrations at home in Detroit. Grandmother documented every day's events in her yearly diary. Supplemented with photos, our celebrations are preserved for generations to come—or simply for our own enjoyment. —MM

My Christmas Diary

CHRISTMAS DAY

_____

YEAR

_____

WHERE CELEBRATED

GUESTS

MENU

_____   _____
_____   _____
_____   _____
_____   _____
_____   _____
_____   _____
_____   _____
_____   _____
_____   _____
_____   _____
_____   _____
_____   _____
_____   _____
_____   _____
_____   _____
_____   _____
_____   _____
_____   _____
_____   _____

'Tis the season to be jolly!

_____

EVENT AND DATE

_____

WHERE   CELEBRATED

GUESTS   MENU

_____   _____

_____   _____

_____   _____

_____   _____

_____   _____

_____   _____

_____   _____

_____   _____

_____   _____

_____   _____

_____   _____

_____   _____

_____   _____

_____   _____

_____   _____

_____   _____

_____   _____

_____   _____

_____   _____

_____   _____

_____   _____

"At Christmas play and make good cheer

EVENT AND DATE

WHERE CELEBRATED

GUESTS

MENU

for Christmas comes but once a year." —Thomas Tusser

November 22 _____

_____

November 23 _____

_____

November 24 _____

_____

November 25 _____

_____

November 26 _____

_____

November 27 _____

_____

November 28 _____

_____

November 29 _____

_____

November 30 _____

_____

December 1 _____

_____

December 2 _____

_____

December 3 _____

_____

December 4 _____

December 5 _____

December 6 _____

December 7 _____

December 8 _____

December 9 _____

December 10 _____

December 11 _____

December 12 _____

December 13 _____

December 14 _____

December 15 _____

theme calendars are welcome gifts.

December 16 _____

December 17 _____

December 18 _____

December 19 _____

December 20 _____

December 21 _____

December 22 _____

December 23 _____

December 24 _____

December 25 _____

_____

_____

_____

_____

_____

When visiting, be prepared for cooler environments.

December 26 _____

December 27 _____

December 28 _____

December 29 _____

December 30 _____

December 31 _____

January 1 _____

January 2 _____

January 3 _____

January 4 _____

January 5 _____

January 6 _____

Replace your winter scarf with a shawl that will complement your outfit.

HOLIDAY CARDS

Sent   *Received* ✓

Renew an old friendship with a

Sent	Received ✓

Christmas greeting and note.

HOLIDAY GIVING

Gift for	Item	Cost

Gifts need not be expensive;

Gift for	Item	Cost

remember, it's the thought that counts.

STUFF FOR STOCKINGS

A stocking for — *Stuffings*

> *Fill stockings for your loved ones with*
>
> ■
>
> *Little sacks of dried fruits or nuts*
>
> ■
>
> *Unusual teas or coffees*
>
> ■
>
> *Tag sale treasures*
>
> ■
>
> *A seashell or pretty rock from your vacation*
>
> ■
>
> *Gift subscription to a specialty publication tied with a bow!*

Stockings are the best part of Christmas!

SHOPPING NOTES

Determine a price range and stick to it.

GIFTS RECEIVED

From	Gift item

Not just what you wanted? Your local charity welcomes donations.

A SPECIAL MOMENT TO REMEMBER

_____

_____

_____

_____

_____

_____

_____

_____

_____

_____

_____

_____

_____

_____

_____

_____

_____

_____

_____

_____

_____

_____

No matter how early my sisters and I snuck downstairs on Christmas morning, Grandma had already been down and the smell of the turkey, roasting in the oven, filled the air. We wondered if she'd seen Santa as they both had "things to do" in the wee hours, but Grandma assured us that when she passed through the living room, the stockings were already filled.

—Christmas morning in the 50's

Jot it down right away and remember it always.

HOLIDAY CRAFT PROJECT

_____

_____

_____

_____

_____

_____

_____

_____

_____

_____

_____

_____

_____

_____

_____

_____

_____

_____

_____

_____

_____

_____

SNOWY PINE CONE TREES

PERFECT FOR MANTEL AND TABLE ARRANGEMENTS,
THEY ALSO MAKE GREAT PARTY FAVORS OR PLACE CARD HOLDERS.

Materials needed:
Assorted pine cones, 3" to 5" tall. Take a walk and gather some.
1" square wooden beads for base (from craft supply store)
White poster paint and small paintbrush
Glue-gun and glue

Using glue gun, secure pine cone to base. Paint "snow" on tips of pine cone. Different varieties of pine cones make a festive forest!

Crafts aren't just for children!

FAVORITE RECIPE

_____
_____
_____
_____
_____
_____
_____
_____
_____
_____
_____
_____
_____
_____
_____
_____
_____
_____
_____
_____
_____
_____
_____

DECORATE YOUR HOLIDAY HAM

BEGIN YOUR CHRISTMAS DINNER WITH A
BEAUTIFULLY DECORATED HAM AND ENJOY THE KUDOS!

Follow instructions on a precooked ham. For a creative presentation, score the ham fat in a diamond pattern and stud diamond centers with whole cloves. Prepare your serving platter with a bed of kale to support a compote of dried fruit such as cranberries, cherries, figs, prunes, or pineapple cooked in apple juice. Arrange fruit on the bed of kale to frame your ham. Drizzle the pan juices over the ham before serving.

Store and serve your holiday cookies in decorative tins.

PHOTOGRAPHS

Be prepared for that precious moment

and have several disposable cameras on hand.

HOTOGRAPHS

Gather disposable cameras as they get used up

and replace with fresh ones!

NOTES

Good times, good friends!

CHRISTMAS DAY

_____
YEAR

_____
WHERE CELEBRATED

GUESTS   MENU

_____   _____

_____   _____

_____   _____

_____   _____

_____   _____

_____   _____

_____   _____

_____   _____

_____   _____

_____   _____

_____   _____

_____   _____

_____   _____

_____   _____

_____   _____

_____   _____

_____   _____

_____   _____

Your warm welcome will lift hearts higher.

_____

EVENT AND DATE

_____

WHERE   CELEBRATED

GUESTS   MENU

_____   _____
_____   _____
_____   _____
_____   _____
_____   _____
_____   _____
_____   _____
_____   _____
_____   _____
_____   _____
_____   _____
_____   _____
_____   _____
_____   _____
_____   _____
_____   _____
_____   _____
_____   _____

Note your options, have alternative plans,

EVENT AND DATE

WHERE CELEBRATED

GUESTS   MENU

_____   _____
_____   _____
_____   _____
_____   _____
_____   _____
_____   _____
_____   _____
_____   _____
_____   _____
_____   _____
_____   _____
_____   _____
_____   _____
_____   _____
_____   _____
_____   _____
_____   _____
_____   _____
_____   _____

and last-minute changes will not daunt you.

November 22 _____

_____

November 23 _____

_____

November 24 _____

_____

November 25 _____

_____

November 26 _____

_____

November 27 _____

_____

November 28 _____

_____

November 29 _____

_____

November 30 _____

_____

December 1 _____

_____

December 2 _____

_____

December 3 _____

_____

December 4 _____

December 5 _____

December 6 _____

December 7 _____

December 8 _____

December 9 _____

December 10 _____

December 11 _____

December 12 _____

December 13 _____

December 14 _____

December 15 _____

children love birthstone gifts.

December 16 ─────────────────────────────

December 17 ─────────────────────────────

December 18 ─────────────────────────────

December 19 ─────────────────────────────

December 20 ─────────────────────────────

December 21 ─────────────────────────────

December 22 ─────────────────────────────

December 23 ─────────────────────────────

December 24 ─────────────────────────────

December 25 ─────────────────────────────

Don't succumb to the temptation

December 26 _____

_____

December 27 _____

_____

December 28 _____

_____

December 29 _____

_____

December 30 _____

_____

December 31 _____

_____

January 1 _____

_____

January 2 _____

_____

January 3 _____

_____

January 4 _____

_____

January 5 _____

_____

January 6 _____

_____

to overbook your time!

HOLIDAY CARDS

Sent	Received ✓

Remember the parents of an old friend

Sent	Received ✓

and include a current photo of yourself.

HOLIDAY GIVING

Gift for	Item	Cost

Listen to yourself and let your intuition

Gift for	Item	Cost

guide and influence your decisions.

STUFF FOR STOCKINGS

A stocking for	Stuffings

> *Fill stockings with useful items such as:*
>
> ■
>
> *A sheet of commemorative postage stamps*
>
> ■
>
> *Prepaid telephone calling card*
>
> ■
>
> *Key ring flashlight*
>
> ■
>
> *Book of car wash tickets*
>
> ■
>
> *Theme desk calendar*

Easy-to-hold kitchen items are great for "older" stockings.

SHOPPING NOTES

The perfect token gift may be plenty!

GIFTS RECEIVED

From	Gift item

A certificate for a facial or manicure is a wonderful gift!

$\mathcal{J}$essie and Anouk experienced their first electric train under the tree at ages 12 and 16. Although amused by the train going around and around, neither cat tried to catch it. One morning I happened to glance in the living room, and there were Jessie and Anouk, attention focused on the silent train just waiting for it to move.

Tabby's antics will be humorous in retrospect! ▪

CHEERFUL LITTLE EGG-BIRDS
DECORATE WITH EGG-BIRDS HUNG FROM TWIGS.

Materials needed:
Twigs to use for feet
Rose thorns for beaks
White glue

Fresh brown eggs
Feathers from craft supply store
X-Axto knife with #11 blade
Glue gun for securing bird feet

Binding wire and wire snippers for hanging loop
Paper punch, a felt-tip pen, and white paper for eyes

For each egg-bird, tap a ⅛" hole in the top of an egg using your X-Acto. Tap another slightly larger hole in the bottom of the egg (this will become one of the leg holes). Blow the contents of the egg out through the larger hole, disposing of the contents. Tap small holes in the egg for wings and tail feathers, and another larger hole for the second foot. Snip twigs for feet and glue feet in place with glue gun. When feet are secured, insert feathers for wings and tail securing with a speck of white glue. In top of head, use white glue to secure a feather and a loop of wire for hanging. Use paper punch to make white "dots" for eyes. Glue in place and draw center with pen. Glue on a nice big thorn for a beak!

Complete a project in an afternoon — not a week!

_____

_____

_____

_____

_____

_____

_____

_____

_____

_____

_____

_____

_____

_____

_____

_____

_____

_____

_____

_____

NO-RECIPE ICING

KEEP A BOWL "GOING" THROUGHOUT THE SEASON!

Start with a cup of sifted powdered sugar. Add liquid (water, cream, orange juice), a tablespoon at a time until it is spreadable. Add a bit of butter to make it glossy and flavoring such as vanilla, orange, or almond, if desired. Refrigerate and keep throughout the season, adding more as needed. Good on graham crackers for a quick treat!

Keep it simple—elaborate if time allows.

PHOTOGRAPHS

Take a holiday group portrait.

It could be next year's holiday card!

PHOTOGRAPHS

Share those great photos

as soon as they get printed!

NOTES

Thoughts to remember...

CHRISTMAS DAY

YEAR

WHERE CELEBRATED

GUESTS   MENU

_____   _____
_____   _____
_____   _____
_____   _____
_____   _____
_____   _____
_____   _____
_____   _____
_____   _____
_____   _____
_____   _____
_____   _____
_____   _____
_____   _____
_____   _____
_____   _____
_____   _____
_____   _____

Enjoy every moment today!

_____

EVENT AND DATE

_____

WHERE   CELEBRATED

GUESTS   MENU

_____   _____
_____   _____
_____   _____
_____   _____
_____   _____
_____   _____
_____   _____
_____   _____
_____   _____
_____   _____
_____   _____
_____   _____
_____   _____
_____   _____
_____   _____
_____   _____
_____   _____
_____   _____
_____   _____

You deserve a quiet moment each day

_____

EVENT AND DATE

_____

WHERE CELEBRATED

GUESTS   MENU

_____   _____
_____   _____
_____   _____
_____   _____
_____   _____
_____   _____
_____   _____
_____   _____
_____   _____
_____   _____
_____   _____
_____   _____
_____   _____
_____   _____
_____   _____
_____   _____
_____   _____
_____   _____
_____   _____
_____   _____
_____   _____
_____   _____

to relax, update lists, reflect, and plan.

HOLIDAY CALENDAR

November 22 _____

_____

November 23 _____

_____

November 24 _____

_____

November 25 _____

_____

November 26 _____

_____

November 27 _____

_____

November 28 _____

_____

November 29 _____

_____

November 30 _____

_____

December 1 _____

_____

December 2 _____

_____

December 3 _____

_____

Seasonal music in upbeat tempos like jazz and gospel

December 4 _____

_____

December 5 _____

_____

December 6 _____

_____

December 7 _____

_____

December 8 _____

_____

December 9 _____

_____

December 10 _____

_____

December 11 _____

_____

December 12 _____

_____

December 13 _____

_____

December 14 _____

_____

December 15 _____

_____

are a refreshing way to get into the spirit!

December 16 _____

_____

December 17 _____

_____

December 18 _____

_____

December 19 _____

_____

December 20 _____

_____

December 21 _____

_____

December 22 _____

_____

December 23 _____

_____

December 24 _____

_____

December 25 _____

_____

_____

_____

_____

_____

Write alternative offers and plans

December 26 _____

_____

December 27 _____

_____

December 28 _____

_____

December 29 _____

_____

December 30 _____

_____

December 31 _____

_____

January 1 _____

_____

January 2 _____

_____

January 3 _____

_____

January 4 _____

_____

January 5 _____

_____

January 6 _____

_____

in a different color, or highlight.

HOLIDAY CARDS

Sent   *Received* ✓

Remember one who has extended you a kindness

Sent	Received ✓

during the year with a note of appreciation.

HOLIDAY GIVING

Gift for	Item	Cost

Exchange your service for an event with that of a friend.

Gift for	Item	Cost

The perfect gift can appear at any time, any place!

STUFF FOR STOCKINGS

A stocking for   *Stuffings*

---

*Fill stockings with
tasty nibbles such as:*

•

*A favorite childhood candy
like atomic fireballs*

•

Toasted nuts

•

Dried fruit mix

•

Handmade chocolates

•

*Sugar-free treats from the
health food store*

Tasty unusual edible treats are always fun to receive.

SHOPPING NOTES

Past gift expenditures need not set a precedent.

GIFTS RECEIVED

From	Gift item

Your favorable response is a gift in itself.

A SPECIAL MOMENT TO REMEMBER

Our parents gathered with friends on New Year's Eve leaving us home with our grandmother. When they arrived back home in the wee hours, four-year-old Helen was found curled up in Daddy's big chair, trying her best to stay awake. Asked what she was doing, Helen responded with authority, "Waiting for the Happy New Year."

Children make wonderful observations.

DECORATE THE CHANDELIER

DECORATE YOUR CHANDELIER
AND KEEP THE TABLE FREE FOR FOOD!

Suggested materials:
Leafless branches, bittersweet, or pine boughs, all about 18" long

Place branches, bittersweet, or pine boughs across the "arms" of your chandelier, creating a wreathlike look. Take care not to touch lighting elements.

Hang small ornaments from the branches as you please. Newspapers spread below the chandelier will hasten cleanup. When the season has passed, newspapers in place, snip the branches, allowing them to fall to the paper below and throw them all away.

Things from nature are inspirational and free for the gathering!

_____

_____

_____

_____

_____

_____

_____

_____

_____

_____

_____

_____

_____

_____

_____

_____

_____

_____

_____

ASSORTED HOLIDAY BREADS

SHOP LOCAL HOLIDAY BAZAARS AND GOURMET SHOPS.

The same folks who put on those wonderful church suppers are the suppliers of baked goods for holiday bake sales and bazaars. Purchase an assortment of goodies to have on hand. Ask which can be frozen and stock up! These little extras can complete a table or buffet with homemade goodness—instantly!

Prepare holiday linens ahead of time and delegate table-setting chores. ▪

HOTOGRAPHS

Double prints are inexpensive. Include

the extras with your thank-you notes.

PHOTOGRAPHS

Discarded greeting card boxes

are the right size to label and store photos.

NOTES

Ideas for next year.

CHRISTMAS DAY

_____

YEAR

_____

WHERE CELEBRATED

GUESTS   MENU

_____   _____
_____   _____
_____   _____
_____   _____
_____   _____
_____   _____
_____   _____
_____   _____
_____   _____
_____   _____
_____   _____
_____   _____
_____   _____
_____   _____
_____   _____
_____   _____
_____   _____
_____   _____

Take a few minutes to clear your mind and collect your thoughts.

EVENT AND DATE

WHERE CELEBRATED

GUESTS

MENU

Looking through photos from a wonderful past celebration

_____

EVENT AND DATE

_____

WHERE CELEBRATED

GUESTS   MENU

_____   _____
_____   _____
_____   _____
_____   _____
_____   _____
_____   _____
_____   _____
_____   _____
_____   _____
_____   _____
_____   _____
_____   _____
_____   _____
_____   _____
_____   _____
_____   _____
_____   _____
_____   _____

can calm nerves and set a positive mood.

November 22 ——————————————————————————————

November 23 ——————————————————————————————

November 24 ——————————————————————————————

November 25 ——————————————————————————————

November 26 ——————————————————————————————

November 27 ——————————————————————————————

November 28 ——————————————————————————————

November 29 ——————————————————————————————

November 30 ——————————————————————————————

December 1 ——————————————————————————————

December 2 ——————————————————————————————

December 3 ——————————————————————————————

From amaryllis to paperwhite narcissus, bulbs for indoor forcing

December 4 ————————————————————————————

December 5 ————————————————————————————

December 6 ————————————————————————————

December 7 ————————————————————————————

December 8 ————————————————————————————

December 9 ————————————————————————————

December 10 ————————————————————————————

December 11 ————————————————————————————

December 12 ————————————————————————————

December 13 ————————————————————————————

December 14 ————————————————————————————

December 15 ————————————————————————————

will provide colorful blooms lasting well into the new year.

December 16 ————————————————————————————

——

December 17 ————————————————————————————

——

December 18 ————————————————————————————

——

December 19 ————————————————————————————

——

December 20 ————————————————————————————

——

December 21 ————————————————————————————

——

December 22 ————————————————————————————

——

December 23 ————————————————————————————

——

December 24 ————————————————————————————

——

December 25 ————————————————————————————

——

——

——

——

When plans must be altered,

December 26 _____

December 27 _____

December 28 _____

December 29 _____

December 30 _____

December 31 _____

January 1 _____

January 2 _____

January 3 _____

January 4 _____

January 5 _____

January 6 _____

advise your hostess right away.

HOLIDAY CARDS

Sent	Received ✓

Add a personal note to long-distance greetings.

Sent	Received ✓

Start right after Thanksgiving!

HOLIDAY GIVING

Gift for	Item	Cost

Keep a drawer or box to store gift purchases

Gift for	Item	Cost

you've made throughout the year.

STUFF FOR STOCKINGS

A stocking for	Stuffings

Fill stockings for outdoors folks with:

- *High energy candy bars from sports store*
- *Heavy-duty hand cream*
- *Ear warmers*
- *Lip balm*
- *Fruit and nut treats*

Open stockings with family and friends, and have a hot beverage in hand!

SHOPPING NOTES

Keep a tally to help stick to your budget.

GIFTS RECEIVED

From	Gift item

Be gracious, be thankful.

_____

_____

_____

_____

_____

_____

_____

_____

_____

_____

_____

_____

_____

_____

_____

_____

_____

_____

_____

_____

_____

_____

_____

_____

I visited my sister one Christmas when I was just out of school. Although I had no money for a present, my sister seemed certain I had something wonderful for her. Always the creative type, I bought some colorful textured yarns and a crochet hook then taught myself to crochet. The product of my efforts was a very funky hat that I believe she has to this day.

Always make time for your loved ones.

TABLE FAVORS

A LITTLE TREAT AT EACH PLACE SETTING
WILL START THE MEAL WITH A SMILE.

Suggested materials:
  Sprigs of holly, pine, twigs
  Self-adhesive stars
  Big gumdrops for the base

Cut holly, pine, or twigs about 3" long and secure stems in a big gumdrop. Use self-adhesive stars to "top" the pine or decorate the twigs. Kids love the festive little touches.

Easy crafts can be used for a season or a day—then thrown away!

FAVORITE RECIPE

HOLIDAY GREEN GELATIN

For deep emerald green gelatin, prepare packaged blue gelatin replacing ½ cup of cold water with ½ cup cola.
The color will be a deep rich green and the effervescence in the cola will add a bubbly tingle. Substitute seltzer for cold water for extra bubbly taste.

Locate and note holiday table decorations early in the month.

 PHOTOGRAPHS

Take plenty of photos!

No need to save the bad ones!

PHOTOGRAPHS

editing a photo with scissors!

NOTES

Tips that worked well.

CHRISTMAS DAY

YEAR

WHERE CELEBRATED

GUESTS   MENU

The season of joy is here!

EVENT AND DATE

WHERE CELEBRATED

GUESTS

MENU

Keep shopping lists in a notebook.

_____

EVENT AND DATE

_____

WHERE CELEBRATED

GUESTS   MENU

_____   _____

_____   _____

_____   _____

_____   _____

_____   _____

_____   _____

_____   _____

_____   _____

_____   _____

_____   _____

_____   _____

_____   _____

_____   _____

_____   _____

_____   _____

_____   _____

_____   _____

_____   _____

_____   _____

A notebook is less likely to get misplaced.

November 22 _____

November 23 _____

November 24 _____

November 25 _____

November 26 _____

November 27 _____

November 28 _____

November 29 _____

November 30 _____

December 1 _____

December 2 _____

December 3 _____

Amaranth, cardamom, yogi teas—

December 4 _____

December 5 _____

December 6 _____

December 7 _____

December 8 _____

December 9 _____

December 10 _____

December 11 _____

December 12 _____

December 13 _____

December 14 _____

December 15 _____

unusual spices and teas are thoughtful house gifts.

December 16 ————————————————————————

December 17 ————————————————————————

December 18 ————————————————————————

December 19 ————————————————————————

December 20 ————————————————————————

December 21 ————————————————————————

December 22 ————————————————————————

December 23 ————————————————————————

December 24 ————————————————————————

December 25 ————————————————————————

A lush poinsettia will brighten a room.

December 26 _____

_____

December 27 _____

_____

December 28 _____

_____

December 29 _____

_____

December 30 _____

_____

December 31 _____

_____

January 1 _____

_____

January 2 _____

_____

January 3 _____

_____

January 4 _____

_____

January 5 _____

_____

January 6 _____

_____

Poinsettias come in white and shades of pink, as well as red.

HOLIDAY CARDS

Sent | *Received* ✓

Self-adhesive stamps save time and your tongue.

Sent	Received ✓

Colorful commemorative stamps add a festive, personal touch.

HOLIDAY GIVING

Gift for	Item	Cost

A small extravagance is a real treat.

Gift for	Item	Cost

Two or three are even better!

A stocking for	Stuffings

Fill a cook's stocking with:

■

Table candles—choose unscented

■

Your own rhubarb-ginger conserve

■

Colorful peppercorns

■

A home-state product like Vermont maple syrup

■

Cooking goggles

■ *A tally of likes and hobbies can help with gift choices.*

SHOPPING NOTES

Avoid the temptation to overspend.

GIFTS RECEIVED

From	Gift item

A luxurious "spa" item is great to give or receive.

A SPECIAL MOMENT TO REMEMBER

_____

_____

_____

_____

_____

_____

_____

_____

_____

_____

_____

_____

_____

_____

_____

_____

_____

_____

_____

_____

_____

_____

_____

_____

We'd just gotten a dishwasher. Mom figured "plate warm" would be ideal for thawing the 25-pound rock-solid frozen turkey and loaded it in. Dad came along, and seeing the odd "plate warm" button aglow, pressed "soak." The water flowed and the dishwasher door locked tight, steam pouring from the edges. "My turkey! My turkey!" Mom shrieked tugging at the door. After completing the "soak" cycle, the turkey was indeed thawed and none the worse for wear. As I recall, those present were sworn to secrecy.

A kitchen disaster can be very funny in retrospect!

HOLIDAY CRAFT PROJECT

FIREPLACE AGLOW

FOR INSTANT AMBIENCE

I love a fire in the fireplace but when entertaining, and there is no time to keep a real fire going, I use candles. Several three-inch wide candles, securely balanced on a few logs, cast a warm glow and burn for many hours. The whiteness of birch logs reflect light beautifully. This is a safe way to use a sealed or unused fireplace.

True creativity is in the results, not the time it took!

GELATIN AMBROSIA

BE PREPARED WITH INGREDIENTS ON HAND.

Prepare gelatin in a flat pan. Drain the liquid from small tins of fruit such as grapes, mandarin oranges, pitted Bing or Royal Anne cherries. Whip a pint of heavy cream, sweeten if you like. When gelatin is set, cut into ¾" cubes and toss with the fruit and whipped cream.

The holiday season can be trying; simple pleasures rule!

PHOTOGRAPHS

Show off those adorable pets!

They are cheerful reminders of good times!

PHOTOGRAPHS

A colorful bow on the collar

will dress up a four-legged family member.

NOTES

Mice nest in storage boxes. Dispose of edible decorations.

CHRISTMAS DAY

_____

YEAR

_____

WHERE CELEBRATED

GUESTS   MENU

_____   _____

_____   _____

_____   _____

_____   _____

_____   _____

_____   _____

_____   _____

_____   _____

_____   _____

_____   _____

_____   _____

_____   _____

_____   _____

_____   _____

_____   _____

_____   _____

_____   _____

_____   _____

_____   _____

Today is for joyful celebration!

_____

EVENT AND DATE

_____

WHERE   CELEBRATED

GUESTS   MENU

_____   _____
_____   _____
_____   _____
_____   _____
_____   _____
_____   _____
_____   _____
_____   _____
_____   _____
_____   _____
_____   _____
_____   _____
_____   _____
_____   _____
_____   _____
_____   _____
_____   _____
_____   _____
_____   _____

Gather ideas and notes jotted here and there

_____

EVENT AND DATE

_____

WHERE CELEBRATED

GUESTS   MENU

_____   _____
_____   _____
_____   _____
_____   _____
_____   _____
_____   _____
_____   _____
_____   _____
_____   _____
_____   _____
_____   _____
_____   _____
_____   _____
_____   _____
_____   _____
_____   _____
_____   _____
_____   _____

and record in your journal.

HOLIDAY CALENDAR

November 22 ————————————————————

November 23 ————————————————————

November 24 ————————————————————

November 25 ————————————————————

November 26 ————————————————————

November 27 ————————————————————

November 28 ————————————————————

November 29 ————————————————————

November 30 ————————————————————

December 1 ————————————————————

December 2 ————————————————————

December 3 ————————————————————

A potted herb such as rosemary, bay, or thyme

December 4 _____

December 5 _____

December 6 _____

December 7 _____

December 8 _____

December 9 _____

December 10 _____

December 11 _____

December 12 _____

December 13 _____

December 14 _____

December 15 _____

is an attractive house plant and useful gift for a cook.

December 16 _____

_____

December 17 _____

_____

December 18 _____

_____

December 19 _____

_____

December 20 _____

_____

December 21 _____

_____

December 22 _____

_____

December 23 _____

_____

December 24 _____

_____

December 25 _____

_____

_____

_____

_____

A "put-up" preserve from your pantry is a lovely gift.

December 26 —————————————————

December 27 —————————————————

December 28 —————————————————

December 29 —————————————————

December 30 —————————————————

December 31 —————————————————

January 1 —————————————————

January 2 —————————————————

January 3 —————————————————

January 4 —————————————————

January 5 —————————————————

January 6 —————————————————

Include the recipe on the label or gift card.

HOLIDAY CARDS

Sent

Received ✓

Hand address dark envelopes with a white "colored" pencil.

Sent	Received ✓

Your old electric pencil sharpener will come in handy!

HOLIDAY GIVING

Gift for	Item	Cost

When in doubt, soaps, candles,

Gift for	Item	Cost

or something delicious will bring a smile!

STUFF FOR STOCKINGS

A stocking for	Stuffings

> Fill gardener's stocking
> with harbingers of Spring:
>
> ■
>
> Bulbs to force
>
> ■
>
> Seeds from
> your own garden
>
> ■
>
> Good gardening gloves
>
> ■
>
> A garden holiday ornament
>
> ■
>
> Special hand soap

A stretchy stocking is more accommodating!

SHOPPING NOTES

Put together your own small gift baskets.

GIFTS RECEIVED

From	Gift item

Jot item received on the gift tag as a reminder for your thank-you notes.

For several years I was fortunate to be a part of a traditional Polish Christmas. On Christmas Eve twelve courses or foods were served representing the twelve apostles. Fruit, fish, soup, vegetables, several kinds of pierogi, opłatek (a wafer shared with all at the table), and assorted holiday cookies. This eclectic group changed from year to year as did the menu—which evolved to the courses being the traditional wafer, several kinds of pierogi with plenty of sour cream and butter, and, of course, lots of cookies. No one left hungry for food or family!

Memories of past celebrations bring peace and joy.

CLOVE BALLS

CLOVE-COVERED FRUIT LASTS FOR YEARS AND IMPROVES WITH AGE.

Best to start early in the season. Remember, all fruit shrinks over time. Purchase cloves in bulk from a co-op, specialty, or health food store. Choose lemons, oranges, limes, or apples. I use a skewer or nail to pierce a hole for each clove—using a thimble to press the clove into the hole will further save your fingertips. Allow to dry for several weeks. Cloves will "tighten up" for solid coverage! Tie each with a ribbon for hanging or group in a bowl. The scent is light but lasts for years.

Enjoy the process! Have all materials needed on hand.

FAVORITE RECIPE

STUFFED DATES

PITTED DATES, NUT MEATS, AND A BOWL OF
GRANULATED SUGAR ARE ALL YOU NEED.

Press a nut meat into the opening left by the pit, then roll stuffed date in sugar.
Dates pack nicely in small boxes for favors or gifts. Keep a tin on hand for company.

Write and attach your recipe as part of your home-baked gift.

PHOTOGRAPHS

Check your camera battery and have a replacement on hand.

An extra roll or two of film may come in handy!

HOTOGRAPHS

Check film for expiration date

to avoid disappointing color.

NOTES

Pass older and unused decorations along to a charity thrift shop.

CHRISTMAS DAY

_____
YEAR

_____
WHERE CELEBRATED

GUESTS   MENU

_____   _____
_____   _____
_____   _____
_____   _____
_____   _____
_____   _____
_____   _____
_____   _____
_____   _____
_____   _____
_____   _____
_____   _____
_____   _____
_____   _____
_____   _____
_____   _____
_____   _____
_____   _____

Be prepared with treats for the little ones!

EVENT AND DATE

WHERE CELEBRATED

GUESTS

MENU

A cache of small, inexpensive items may come in handy

_____

EVENT AND DATE

_____

WHERE CELEBRATED

GUESTS   MENU

_____   _____

_____   _____

_____   _____

_____   _____

_____   _____

_____   _____

_____   _____

_____   _____

_____   _____

_____   _____

_____   _____

_____   _____

_____   _____

_____   _____

_____   _____

_____   _____

_____   _____

_____   _____

to calm or entertain an overexcited child.

November 22 _____

_____

November 23 _____

_____

November 24 _____

_____

November 25 _____

_____

November 26 _____

_____

November 27 _____

_____

November 28 _____

_____

November 29 _____

_____

November 30 _____

_____

December 1 _____

_____

December 2 _____

_____

December 3 _____

_____

Seasonal music especially for children

December 4 _____

_____

December 5 _____

_____

December 6 _____

_____

December 7 _____

_____

December 8 _____

_____

December 9 _____

_____

December 10 _____

_____

December 11 _____

_____

December 12 _____

_____

December 13 _____

_____

December 14 _____

_____

December 15 _____

_____

will cheer and entertain both young and young at heart.

December 16 _____

_____

December 17 _____

_____

December 18 _____

_____

December 19 _____

_____

December 20 _____

_____

December 21 _____

_____

December 22 _____

_____

December 23 _____

_____

December 24 _____

_____

December 25 _____

_____

_____

_____

_____

A holiday ornament for your hostess will commemorate the event.

December 26 _____

_____

December 27 _____

_____

December 28 _____

_____

December 29 _____

_____

December 30 _____

_____

December 31 _____

_____

January 1 _____

_____

January 2 _____

_____

January 3 _____

_____

January 4 _____

_____

January 5 _____

_____

January 6 _____

_____

Allow a child the honor of placing it on the tree!

HOLIDAY CARDS

Sent   *Received* ✓

Print mailing labels on clear label stock.

Sent	Received ✓

They will "disappear" on any color envelope.

HOLIDAY GIVING

Gift for	Item	Cost

A list of favorite things, favorite colors, or hobbies

Gift for	Item	Cost

will help when shopping for children!

STUFF FOR STOCKINGS

A stocking for	Stuffings

Fill a stocking with
treasures such as:
■
Special photo
in a tiny frame
■
Funky jewelry from a
thrift shop or flea market
■
Humorous pen or key ring
■
Dime store novelty toys

Stockings of equal size will avoid squabbles among children.

SHOPPING NOTES

Fun-to-play learning games for kids have staying power!

GIFTS RECEIVED

From	Gift item

A gift certificate to a favorite store or a health club will be used!

A SPECIAL MOMENT TO REMEMBER ▪

As children we were served holiday meals at a card table in the sun room. Adults filled the dining room to capacity and we had to shift for ourselves after the first round of food was passed. I remember being left out of the dessert circuit one year. Wedged in a corner, I managed to wiggle out and head for the kitchen where a choice of plum or suet pudding, with either vanilla or lemon sauce, awaited. It didn't matter which I took as long as it was swimming with vanilla sauce. My dessert bowl brimming and a cup of tea in my other hand, I wiggled back into my place at the card table. Preparing to savor that first big bite of pudding, I opened wide, closed my eyes, and YIKES! I'd managed to drench my pudding in turkey gravy!

Document and share your special memories. ▪

_____

_____

_____

_____

_____

_____

_____

_____

_____

_____

_____

_____

_____

_____

_____

_____

_____

WRAPPING A BIG GIFT

LARGE GIFTS USE A LOT OF GIFT WRAP—
HERE IS AN EASY ALTERNATIVE:

Kraft paper can be elegant! Purchase kraft paper in a roll, soap erasers (the crumbly ones), and white poster paint.

Using an X-Axto knife, cut a shape into the soft soap eraser— a star, a snowflake, a holly sprig. Draw the shape on first if you choose. Trim away the eraser edges, leaving the raised shape intact. Wrap gift then use soap eraser stamp and white paint as you would a stamp and stamp pad. Stamp at random! White poster paint is thick, dries opaque, and contrasts nicely against the brown paper.

Store your craft necessities in a clearly marked box or tin.

FAVORITE RECIPE

_____
_____
_____
_____
_____
_____
_____
_____
_____
_____
_____
_____
_____
_____
_____
_____
_____
_____
_____
_____
_____
_____

PERK UP THE GREEN BEANS

OH, NO! NOT GREEN BEAN CASSEROLE!

It appears to be a tradition in itself—green bean casserole. Improve upon Mom's and make a real white sauce. Include toasted slivered almonds and top with crushed toasted almonds mixed with bread crumbs.

Transport food-to-bring in a container to leave as a gift for the host.

HOTOGRAPHS

and save with your holiday menu.

PHOTOGRAPHS

for a great photo—it's well worth the effort!

NOTES

Enjoy the catalogs, shop the off-price stores—you may be surprised!

CHRISTMAS DAY

_____

YEAR

_____

WHERE CELEBRATED

GUESTS   MENU

_____   _____

_____   _____

_____   _____

_____   _____

_____   _____

_____   _____

_____   _____

_____   _____

_____   _____

_____   _____

_____   _____

_____   _____

_____   _____

_____   _____

_____   _____

_____   _____

_____   _____

_____   _____

Less is more — keep it simple.

_____

EVENT AND DATE

_____

WHERE   CELEBRATED

GUESTS   MENU

_____   _____
_____   _____
_____   _____
_____   _____
_____   _____
_____   _____
_____   _____
_____   _____
_____   _____
_____   _____
_____   _____
_____   _____
_____   _____
_____   _____
_____   _____
_____   _____
_____   _____
_____   _____
_____   _____

Take a break, put your feet up

EVENT AND DATE

WHERE CELEBRATED

GUESTS   MENU

and enjoy a moment of well-deserved satisfaction.

November 22 _____

_____

November 23 _____

_____

November 24 _____

_____

November 25 _____

_____

November 26 _____

_____

November 27 _____

_____

November 28 _____

_____

November 29 _____

_____

November 30 _____

_____

December 1 _____

_____

December 2 _____

_____

December 3 _____

_____

Useful gifts such as decorative notepad cubes

December 4 ———————————————————————

———————————————————————————————————

December 5 ———————————————————————

———————————————————————————————————

December 6 ———————————————————————

———————————————————————————————————

December 7 ———————————————————————

———————————————————————————————————

December 8 ———————————————————————

———————————————————————————————————

December 9 ———————————————————————

———————————————————————————————————

December 10 ——————————————————————

———————————————————————————————————

December 11 ——————————————————————

———————————————————————————————————

December 12 ——————————————————————

———————————————————————————————————

December 13 ——————————————————————

———————————————————————————————————

December 14 ——————————————————————

———————————————————————————————————

December 15 ——————————————————————

———————————————————————————————————

and pens are always well received.

December 16 _____

_____

December 17 _____

_____

December 18 _____

_____

December 19 _____

_____

December 20 _____

_____

December 21 _____

_____

December 22 _____

_____

December 23 _____

_____

December 24 _____

_____

December 25 _____

_____

_____

_____

_____

_____

Miniature twinkle lights at your entryway

December 26 _____

December 27 _____

December 28 _____

December 29 _____

December 30 _____

December 31 _____

January 1 _____

January 2 _____

January 3 _____

January 4 _____

January 5 _____

January 6 _____

add a festive welcome to visitors.

HOLIDAY CARDS

Sent | *Received* ✓

Express your appreciation for a past kindness

Sent	Received ✓

or favor with a holiday card and note.

HOLIDAY GIVING

Gift for	Item	Cost

Give a gift you'd love to receive —

Gift for	Item	Cost

the concept may be contageous!

STUFF FOR STOCKINGS

A stocking for	Stuffings

Stuffers for a reader may include:

■

Bookmarks

■

Pocket magnifier or magnifying half-glasses

■

Gift subscription to a literary journal

■

Daylight or full-spectrum lightbulbs

Hide a big stocking stuffer and "stuff" a card telling where to look!

SHOPPING NOTES

If you love it, chances are a friend will, too!

GIFTS RECEIVED

From	Gift item

Graciously receive an unexpected gift—your thank-you is a welcome response.

_____

_____

_____

_____

_____

_____

_____

_____

_____

_____

_____

_____

_____

_____

_____

_____

_____

_____

_____

_____

_____

_____

A tradition at our home was having Santa visit us on Christmas evening with a little present for each family member. Uncle George, who was of convincing size, surreptitiously donned the Santa suit, loaded the gifts in a pillowcase, and rapped on the front door. The children welcomed him with squeals of delight, and he proceeded to read the names on tags and dole out the gifts. He'd wish us all a "Merry Christmas" and head out the front door. My older sister, about five years old at the time, urged Santa to "Go up the chimney!" Glancing at the fire ablaze in the fireplace, "Santa" gave a deep sigh and said he'd been up and down chimneys all night and day. The considerate little Catherine nodded and led him politely to the front door.

Childhood memories last forever. ▪

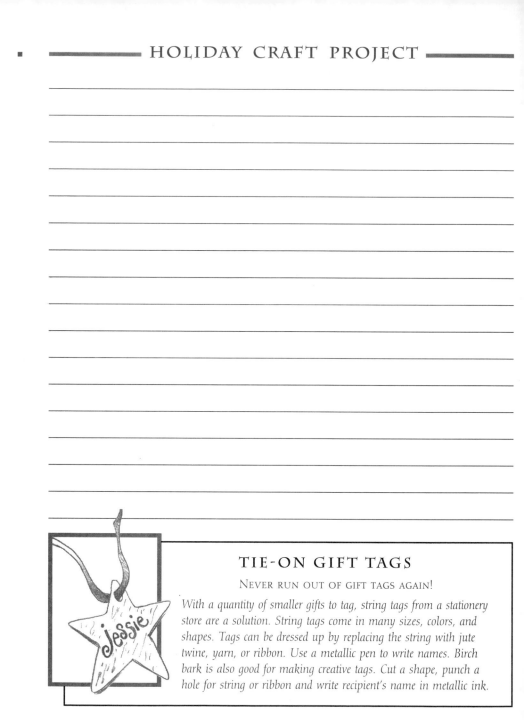

TIE-ON GIFT TAGS

NEVER RUN OUT OF GIFT TAGS AGAIN!

With a quantity of smaller gifts to tag, string tags from a stationery store are a solution. String tags come in many sizes, colors, and shapes. Tags can be dressed up by replacing the string with jute twine, yarn, or ribbon. Use a metallic pen to write names. Birch bark is also good for making creative tags. Cut a shape, punch a hole for string or ribbon and write recipient's name in metallic ink.

Buy several pair of small scissors and always have a pair handy.

LEMON CUPS

THIS COMFORT FOOD HAS A CAKELIKE TOP AND PUDDING BELOW.

In a medium-size bowl, beat 3 egg whites. When egg whites are stiff, beat in 3 tablespoons of sugar. In a large bowl beat 3 egg yolks. When egg yolks are light in color, beat in ¾ cup plus 1 tablespoon sugar, 4 tablespoons flour, ⅛ teaspoon salt, 5 tablespoons lemon juice (juice of one big lemon), 1½ cups milk, and 2 tablespoons melted butter. Fold egg whites into yolk mix. Pour into 6 greased custard cups and set cups in a pan of water. Bake at 350°F for about 1 hour.

Add a festive touch to an old favorite.

PHOTOGRAPHS

Photograph the tree as soon as it is decorated

and preserve the perfection.

PHOTOGRAPHS

at dusk with the window "candles" lit.

NOTES

CHRISTMAS DAY

YEAR

WHERE CELEBRATED

GUESTS

MENU

Enjoy last year's holiday photos!

_____

EVENT AND DATE

_____

WHERE CELEBRATED

GUESTS   MENU

_____   _____
_____   _____
_____   _____
_____   _____
_____   _____
_____   _____
_____   _____
_____   _____
_____   _____
_____   _____
_____   _____
_____   _____
_____   _____
_____   _____
_____   _____
_____   _____
_____   _____
_____   _____

A favor or kindness to a friend or stranger

EVENT AND DATE

WHERE CELEBRATED

GUESTS   MENU

_____   _____
_____   _____
_____   _____
_____   _____
_____   _____
_____   _____
_____   _____
_____   _____
_____   _____
_____   _____
_____   _____
_____   _____
_____   _____
_____   _____
_____   _____
_____   _____
_____   _____
_____   _____
_____   _____

will warm two hearts.

November 22 ─────────────────────────────────

───

November 23 ─────────────────────────────────

───

November 24 ─────────────────────────────────

───

November 25 ─────────────────────────────────

───

November 26 ─────────────────────────────────

───

November 27 ─────────────────────────────────

───

November 28 ─────────────────────────────────

───

November 29 ─────────────────────────────────

───

November 30 ─────────────────────────────────

───

December 1 ──────────────────────────────────

───

December 2 ──────────────────────────────────

───

December 3 ──────────────────────────────────

───

Pets are "family" to many adults.

December 4 ———————————————————

December 5 ———————————————————

December 6 ———————————————————

December 7 ———————————————————

December 8 ———————————————————

December 9 ———————————————————

December 10 ———————————————————

December 11 ———————————————————

December 12 ———————————————————

December 13 ———————————————————

December 14 ———————————————————

December 15 ———————————————————

Remembering "Socks" or "Boots" will please both pet and human.

December 16 ————————————————————————

———————————————————————————————————————

December 17 ————————————————————————

———————————————————————————————————————

December 18 ————————————————————————

———————————————————————————————————————

December 19 ————————————————————————

———————————————————————————————————————

December 20 ————————————————————————

———————————————————————————————————————

December 21 ————————————————————————

———————————————————————————————————————

December 22 ————————————————————————

———————————————————————————————————————

December 23 ————————————————————————

———————————————————————————————————————

December 24 ————————————————————————

———————————————————————————————————————

December 25 ————————————————————————

———————————————————————————————————————

———————————————————————————————————————

———————————————————————————————————————

———————————————————————————————————————

———————————————————————————————————————

With the abundance of sweets,

December 26 _____

_____

December 27 _____

_____

December 28 _____

_____

December 29 _____

_____

December 30 _____

_____

December 31 _____

_____

January 1 _____

_____

January 2 _____

_____

January 3 _____

_____

January 4 _____

_____

January 5 _____

_____

January 6 _____

_____

fill a candy bowl with fruit gels and sours.

HOLIDAY CARDS

Sent

Received ✓

Many charities offer holiday cards to benefit their programs.

Sent	Received ✓

Or, in lieu of cards, donate directly to your favorite charity.

HOLIDAY GIVING

Gift for	Item	Cost

Be sure gifts for pets are safe and nontoxic.

Gift for	Item	Cost

Use nontoxic wrappings, too!

STUFF FOR STOCKINGS

A stocking for	Stuffings

Stuffers for a favorite pet:

■

Pet treats or cookies

■

*Silly toys—just look
in the pet aisle!*

■

*Fresh catnip
or chewy bones*

■

*Donation to their "alma
mater" (Humane Society,
shelter, breed association)*

Stocking items for pets are easy to shop for.

SHOPPING NOTES

A little fresh catnip goes a long way!

GIFTS RECEIVED

From	Gift item

Remember a gift of time or assistance with a note of thanks and appreciation.

_____
_____
_____
_____
_____
_____
_____
_____
_____
_____
_____
_____
_____
_____
_____
_____
_____
_____
_____
_____
_____
_____
_____
_____

> _The table was set, candles lit, and the wine and water glasses filled. No one noticed Admiral Byrd, the parakeet, was out for a holiday fly and having a nip—choosing wine over water. When the family gathered at the table, the Admiral was tail feathers up in a glass of wine! We managed to revive him but, as I recall, not much turkey was eaten that Christmas!_

Look for the humor and have a laugh!

PINE NEEDLE PRESENTS

RECYCLE YOUR WREATH INTO SACHETS OR PILLOWS.

If you sew, this is a project for you. Save the pine needles from your Christmas wreath by crumbling them onto a newspaper and pouring into a bag for storage. Use the cache for filling sachets and small pillows of your own making. Line pillows to soften the touch and keep needles from coming through the fabric. Velvets, velveteens, brocades, and tapestries lend themselves to decorative braided trims, fringe, and tassels. The delicate natural pine scent within will last for years.

Give your craft decorations to those who admire them!

FAVORITE RECIPE

SNOWBALLS

EASY AND FESTIVE, SNOWBALLS DELIGHT CHILDREN.

Roll round scoops of vanilla ice cream or pineapple sorbet in a bowl of angel-flake coconut. Serve in sorbet cups or on a dessert plate with a dusting of coconut "snow-flakes." For smaller snowballs, use a melon-ball scoop.

Paper doilies add a festive touch to dessert.

PHOTOGRAPHS

and include all the pets!

When photographing pets, use a treat to encourage cooperation.

This works well for people, too!

NOTES

Cats appreciate a quiet place away from the excitement.

CHRISTMAS DAY

_____

YEAR

_____

WHERE CELEBRATED

GUESTS   MENU

_____   _____
_____   _____
_____   _____
_____   _____
_____   _____
_____   _____
_____   _____
_____   _____
_____   _____
_____   _____
_____   _____
_____   _____
_____   _____
_____   _____
_____   _____
_____   _____
_____   _____

Thoughtfulness is priceless.

_____

EVENT AND DATE

_____

WHERE   CELEBRATED

GUESTS   MENU

_____   _____
_____   _____
_____   _____
_____   _____
_____   _____
_____   _____
_____   _____
_____   _____
_____   _____
_____   _____
_____   _____
_____   _____
_____   _____
_____   _____
_____   _____
_____   _____
_____   _____
_____   _____

A helping hand may be more welcome

_____

EVENT AND DATE

_____

WHERE CELEBRATED

GUESTS   MENU

_____   _____

_____   _____

_____   _____

_____   _____

_____   _____

_____   _____

_____   _____

_____   _____

_____   _____

_____   _____

_____   _____

_____   _____

_____   _____

_____   _____

_____   _____

_____   _____

_____   _____

_____   _____

than a purchased gift.

HOLIDAY CALENDAR

November 22 ———————————————————————————

———————————————————————————————————————

November 23 ———————————————————————————

———————————————————————————————————————

November 24 ———————————————————————————

———————————————————————————————————————

November 25 ———————————————————————————

———————————————————————————————————————

November 26 ———————————————————————————

———————————————————————————————————————

November 27 ———————————————————————————

———————————————————————————————————————

November 28 ———————————————————————————

———————————————————————————————————————

November 29 ———————————————————————————

———————————————————————————————————————

November 30 ———————————————————————————

———————————————————————————————————————

December 1 ————————————————————————————

———————————————————————————————————————

December 2 ————————————————————————————

———————————————————————————————————————

December 3 ————————————————————————————

———————————————————————————————————————

A fruit-of-the-month-type gift will be most welcome

December 4 _____

December 5 _____

December 6 _____

December 7 _____

December 8 _____

December 9 _____

December 10 _____

December 11 _____

December 12 _____

December 13 _____

December 14 _____

December 15 _____

to a housebound friend or relative.

December 16 _____

_____

December 17 _____

_____

December 18 _____

_____

December 19 _____

_____

December 20 _____

_____

December 21 _____

_____

December 22 _____

_____

December 23 _____

_____

December 24 _____

_____

December 25 _____

_____

_____

_____

_____

Modify plans when the weather gets nasty.

December 26 ———————————————————

———————————————————

December 27 ———————————————————

———————————————————

December 28 ———————————————————

———————————————————

December 29 ———————————————————

———————————————————

December 30 ———————————————————

———————————————————

December 31 ———————————————————

———————————————————

January 1 ———————————————————

———————————————————

January 2 ———————————————————

———————————————————

January 3 ———————————————————

———————————————————

January 4 ———————————————————

———————————————————

January 5 ———————————————————

———————————————————

January 6 ———————————————————

———————————————————

Canceling an event may be the wise and prudent decision.

HOLIDAY CARDS

Sent   *Received* ✓

For an extensive list of relatives,

Sent	Received ✓

include a reprint of one great family photo.

HOLIDAY GIVING

Gift for	Item	Cost

Gifts stored in hiding places are easily forgotten.

Gift for	Item	Cost

Designate a "hands off" closet or drawer—lock if necessary!

STUFF FOR STOCKINGS

A stocking for	Stuffings

Stuffers to pamper include:
- Dried rosebud sachet
- Lightly scented candles
- Pocket-size moisturizer
- Sample-size beauty supplies
- Sleeping gloves and hand cream

Include clementines and pistachios in every stocking!

SHOPPING NOTES

Buy decorations at a discount store to donate—nice, inexpensive, and new!

GIFTS RECEIVED

From	Gift item

Enjoy every moment. Memories are gifts to cherish.

A SPECIAL MOMENT TO REMEMBER

A dear friend of mine, in the catering business, was a wonderful host. I arrived at one of his gatherings quite hungry and was surprised to see dinner not yet started. Fritz had Brazilian music playing, decorations up from his recent trip, and a stack of photos in a festive bowl. He told of his adventures while preparing dinner and soon hunger was lost to laughter and a helping hand as Fritz's entertaining style involved us all. I cannot remember a thing we ate but the evening was delightful! Fritz always said, "It's your hospitality that will be remembered." I think of Fritz whenever I have guests.

When entertaining, it's your hospitality that will be remembered!

GARLANDS FROM NATURE

PINE CONES, SPRIGS OF PINE, AND ACORNS
ARE EASILY MADE INTO GARLANDS.

Pine cones and acorns with leaves attached are particularly pretty. You'll need jute twine, narrow ribbon for bows, and a glue gun with glue sticks.

Place jute twine the length of your garland, with a hanging loop at each end, on a flat surface. Cut jute or narrow ribbon in lengths to make small bows. Tie bows to pine cones, acorn stems, or sprigs of pine. Next, evenly space—about 6" apart—against the garland proper and glue to jute twine. Your imagination rules!

Work on newspapers or kraft paper for easy cleanup.

FAVORITE RECIPE

CRANBERRY ORANGE FREEZE

HAVE ON HAND FOR AN INSTEAD-OF-ICE-CREAM MOMENT.

Wash and remove stems from packaged fresh cranberries. Wash and cut an orange into small pieces. Blend both in a food processor along with ¾ cup of sugar and a cup of orange juice until finely chopped. Pour into a flat pan and freeze. Serve in squares. Stays firm for about half an hour.

Save tins and boxes to package gift food items.

PHOTOGRAPHS

Use photos disk to create next year's Christmas card.

Put your favorite photo on your holiday web page!

PHOTOGRAPHS

Stash a couple of disposable cameras in the kitchen

for yourself and your busy helpers!

NOTES

Note quantity choices—too much or too little?

Special Celebrations

HOLIDAY SEASON
BIRTHDAY REMEMBRANCES

Birthday celebrant	Date	Event

Celebrate a personal special day always!

A FIRST CHRISTMAS
BIRTHDAY CELEBRATION

_____

Birthday Baby

_____

Year

_____

_____

_____

_____

_____

_____

_____

_____

_____

_____

_____

_____

_____

_____

_____

_____

_____

_____

List those in attendance and what gifts baby received.

CHRISTMAS BIRTHDAYS

Birthday Celebrant: _____ Year _____
Special acknowledgment _____
_____

Birthday Celebrant: _____ Year _____
Special acknowledgment _____
_____

Birthday Celebrant: _____ Year _____
Special acknowledgment _____
_____

Birthday Celebrant: _____ Year _____
Special acknowledgment _____
_____

Birthday Celebrant: _____ Year _____
Special acknowledgment _____
_____

Birthday Celebrant: _____ Year _____
Special acknowledgment _____
_____

Remember a Christmas birthday with something special.

SPECIAL GATHERINGS

A Reunion of Cousins for the Children

_____

Year

_____

_____

_____

_____

_____

_____

_____

_____

_____

_____

_____

_____

_____

_____

_____

_____

_____

_____

_____

_____

_____

_____

Share photos of when their aunts and uncles were their age.

A Gathering of Young Friends

_____

Year

_____

_____

_____

_____

_____

_____

_____

_____

_____

_____

_____

_____

_____

_____

_____

_____

_____

_____

_____

_____

_____

_____

Read aloud a holiday story and have token "theme" favors.

SPECIAL GATHERINGS

A Gathering of Neighbors

_____

Year

_____

_____

_____

_____

_____

_____

_____

_____

_____

_____

_____

_____

_____

_____

_____

_____

_____

_____

_____

_____

_____

_____

Friendship opportunities abound!

SPECIAL GATHERINGS

A Reunion of School or Workplace friends

_____

Year

_____

_____

_____

_____

_____

_____

_____

_____

_____

_____

_____

_____

_____

_____

_____

_____

_____

_____

_____

_____

_____

_____

As years pass, the memories will be cherished.

SPECIAL GATHERINGS

A Musical Outing

_____

Year

_____

_____

_____

_____

_____

_____

_____

_____

_____

_____

_____

_____

_____

_____

_____

_____

_____

_____

_____

_____

_____

Caroling or an evening at the Nutcracker—create a musical event.